SEEDS OF A SUNFLOWER:

DREA

DEDICATION

To all those who inspired and encouraged me to be creative, think outside the box, and find my identity.

TABLE OF CONTENTS

CYCLE I: THE SOIL

Stop Surviving and Start Living

-A FRIEND

EMBRACE YOUR TRAUMA

Trauma, a word associated with drama
Taught in society to be ashamed
Of what you went through
To be associated with your name
But these situations made you.

Working through your trauma is brave
Your mental health is sabotaged
Thinking it's imagined like a mirage
But you overcame those obstacles.

So challenging, but you survived and stayed alive
And no one knows the sacrifices you chose
Like the phoenix, you rose, and you can't be stopped.

Trauma tries to be a scar forever defining you
Trying you with triggers of emotions and feeling
But there is no reason to hide

It defines who you are—
the abuse, the pain, the rejection, the reflection
No perfection; it's not anything to be ashamed
Your journey is to be respected, elevated, inspired,
desired, courageous.

Contagious, especially when it wasn't the safest
It's a constant reminder of the things you been through,
but it's up to you where the path to recovery takes you.

Reflection seed:

Trauma, by definition, is an emotional response to a terrible event. I didn't hear it as much until I got older-- in my 30s when I started self-reflection, therapy, and what felt normal wasn't so after a while. But things I had been taught to believe were every day. I couldn't ignore it anymore and needed to figure out what it all meant.

FEAR... WHAT ARE YOU?

Fear has no face
Yet somehow, it looks at you daily.
Vibrating through your soul, finding that black hole
I feel seen.

Fear has no name
You can identify it and connect with it
Recognizing without verbalizing
What should I call you?

What are you fear?
How do you know what paralyzes me?
Nobody can see, but you see
You always catch me slipping.

For the last time, fear, we are breaking up
Stop letting me use you as a crutch
Damn you fear; you really suck
But I got something for you.

Afraid of dying, but I keep living
May go broke but still giving
You cripple me, but I rise and walk
O' fear is that all you got?
To talk that talk.

Fear, with no face and no name
Must be lonely, you phony
There is no place for you here
For the last damn time, go away, fear.

Reflection seed:

A moment in time where I felt held hostage, so many things I wanted to do but was afraid to try. I would literally be stuck in a place where fear kept me bound by all the what-ifs... The brain is a powerful tool and the only voice you directly hear all day long. I felt like I needed to talk to this emotion; the voice of fear was creating and keeping me stuck in one place.

P.T.S.D

Push Through Strength & Determination
Praying Through Spiritual Development
Prosperity To Soar and Drive
Prepared not To Stand Down

PTSD, no one can see you but me
In the crowds, the noise gets so loud
But I am alone
And the loud noises trigger me
Oh no, PTSD
Going to kick your butt to the best of my ability

PTSD; day after day, I take a piece of myself back
You try with an anxiety attack
But I'm cool; I'm not going to snap
Because that means you win and I don't lose

Lack of sleep I refuse

Meditation, journaling, grounding tools I use
You met your match in this girl-to-woman, you may be here to stay, but I say go away, PTSD.

You are done, and I won't be sad because I won!

Reflection seed:
A mental condition doesn't define you, and with PTSD, I initially allowed it to control me mentally and physically. My body would continue to let me know that it needed something I wasn't giving it. Once I listened and responded, things took a different turn. I will never ignore the signs again. Also, taking medication isn't sour-- whether it be for your brain or your body because all of it is a part of healing.

EMOTIONAL MATH

People multiply
Adding knowledge
Subtracting negativity
But the hurt divides...

I'm no mathematician, but I know numbers
If one plus one doesn't equal two, then one minus one equals me
Do the problems add up? Are you losing or gaining probability?
But isn't your worth more significant than your hurt?
Do you feel less than and not know that you come first...?

Yet still, emotional math is a subject we all take
Passing and failing daily with no tutor
But you still learn that what doesn't add to your life is subtracting from it.

Multiplying your family, friends, and enemies' bank accounts
But the hurt divides

I say this not to be a negative but as a positive force
Because in life, two negatives don't equal a positive

Your choice of emotional math in this course
It can only add up to what it means ... to live
Don't you know that problems have solutions?
But only if you show and put in the work-- not sacrificing your self-worth

Adding to your life
Subtracting the haters
Multiplying abundance
Dividing and diversifying your paper

Carrying that one and moving that decimal
Your abundance is greater...
Learn your emotional math

Reflection seed:

This was one of the first poems I wrote as I tried to figure out my style. I always heard others say that if someone isn't adding to your life, they are subtracting from it. Something to that degree, but I asked myself how that applied to my life...to going through my emotions as I went through therapy and trying to figure out what that meant... emotional math.

TO BE FREE

A state of mind
Feeling of entrapment
Are you breaking down or breaking through?
Leaving those thoughts of incarceration behind
Freedom, how do I know that it is you?

I walk in freedom, talk in freedom
But why am I still feeling like a hostage
Ability to deliberate, appreciate but not participate
I still feel I held down; freedom, is that you?

Do you know where you're going... I am showing you...
there's more to life
But freedom, how can I be one with you...
My skin, eyes, hair, senses, can I not be free?
Why can't I be what I want to be?

Oh, I see... it's me, only me...

Hold me back... don't disturb, don't rock the boat

Don't I get a vote...

Oh, I get a vote.

It is my life, my choice.

Doesn't anybody else see? Oh, now I see...

The best gift in life is to be free.

Reflection seed:

I found myself trapped within my mind wondering if my choices would affect me. This is what I think goes inside me during an anxiety attack. Anxiety, while something that is occasionally for some, used to be paralyzing for me.

MY FUTURE BORN UNBORN CHILD

Your life is going to be altered in ways you never experienced
The love I have for you is endless
Signs of affection may seem countless;
I have been waiting all my life for you.

The smile-- the attention, the warmth, and concern... worries-- protected by me.
This home I have for you will be the best that you ever seen
I may not shower you with gifts in the physical form but mental and spiritual to help you grow, my future born-unborn child
Do you know I loved you even before I knew you?
That your life before is not the life that I have planned for you?

The hurt and pain you are currently experiencing will be healed by my protection affection.
Reflecting on my pain keeps me more protective of your well-being
I may not have birthed my future unborn child, but as if I birthed you...you are my son or daughter.

Your space to be safe is in my place where only love is allowed
To grow
To know you are loved
To show what you are made of
Whatever you want to be, it is so, and no one can stop that journey but us.

My future born, unborn child...you are the sparkle in my eyes
The feeling in my soul that makes me rise
Happier than the sunrise every morning
You bring me joy.

I can't wait to see you, love you, care for you, be there for you, and share my life with you;
My story made to teach you how powerful you are...my shining star
No one can dim the skies of your bright sunshine
Till we meet soon, my future born-unborn child.

Reflection seed:

Childbirth is considered part of the journey of adulthood—especially motherhood, and sometimes the ability is not within every person's control, whether naturally or through other means. I experienced heartbreak in not being able to carry a child physically. Then I realized that many children are out there without homes seeking that love. I also realized that I am still capable of being a parent to whomever those children are. This poem-letter reminds me that I can still be a mother and have that ability to give love.

CYCLE II: THE SEED

It is important that you decide vs. what you decide.

- MY BIG BROTHER JWIL

A FOREVER CHANGED WOMAN

Tears in your eyes, in the bathroom
Breathing shallow in silence
Just 2 minutes... you will be ok...right?
A splash of water, back to the grind in the spotlight.

Cramps in your body, oh to be a woman
Bleeding from within, mood swings but still walking that walk
Are you ok? Fine, you say...
But not really.

Motherly instinct; your internal clock is ticking
But the battery died, time stopped
There is no reset, sonograms, or heartbeats
Undergo surgery to avoid being buried six feet.

But young woman, why me?
Why me?
The social path has ended
You have been diverted, not knowing what life really is.

A forever changed woman, you are a fighter
A survivor, there is none-- yet many-- like her
A doctor took the last of what she thought her life was... how could this be?
No baby.

Yes maybe... oh, young woman
You still have love to give, an adopted kid; love knows no blood or DNA
Just a loved one, a beautiful place to stay... just wait...
Your journey will be your way to becoming a forever changed woman.

Reflection seed:

Since I can't have children through natural means, this was my pep talk to myself on how I could come out on the other side. A true look into the physical portion of how I found out I couldn't have children and what it felt like constantly breaking down and grieving.

HURT DEVOTION

Am I having a stroke?
Face feeling frozen, brain in love lockdown
Channeling emotions of pain, anxiety, heartbreak, and spending nights awake.
Time doesn't slow down.

Walking that line, the shell of a soul
My heart beats but doesn't feel whole
Grief... oh, the pain of grief
When a relationship ends.

Tears, why are you always here...
I didn't ask for you.
But you always come uninvited.
That feeling of losing breath.

Slowing steps
Fine, I will cry... but why?

Hug me, hold me,
Listen, look at me.

Silence...my thoughts creep
Has it been months, oh...only weeks?
I hurt... stop this pain; I'm drained...
Close my eyes.

Bed holding me hostage, appetite gone
I eat no food, filling empty space just to remain alive...
trying to survive the hurt.

Reflection seed:

Many life changes happened during this period, and it felt like I couldn't move. I felt like I needed to cry for no reason, my joints in my body couldn't work, and I felt paralyzed. It had felt like the worst day of my life and that I wouldn't get through. The human body is truly resilient. Everything is temporary but writing this, it felt like I was in a dark place and that there wasn't any other way out of this.

IDENTITYCRISIS

My name is...
What? Oh, that's the official name, but who am I? A
person, yes, but this may sound silly...

Feeling a case of amnesia.
Looking in the mirror
Reflecting, checking is that me...it couldn't be...

Crisis of identity
But who do I want to be?
A stranger, a person, a leader, a human being
Oh, I see; what I want to be.

Authentic, philanthropic, happy, healthy, majestic
A queen with no throne, a mind of her own—
Oh, hell yeah, that's me!
Feel that energy! Oh, shit, I found it; where you been?
Oh, identity, yes, it's me!

That girl, that woman strong in her walk, a gem, crawl girl
you got this… walk girl… slay sis.

Swag on a drip; haters can't resist
Begone, identity crisis, you done for
Get out, let me in… to be the real one.

Strength to stand tall!
Oh, I know it is me y'all!

Reflection seed:
To be you is to know who you are and what that means to yourself. I didn't know myself; I thought I knew myself, but I only knew a shell of myself. We tend to put on a mask to pretend to be okay when we aren't, and that is when the reflection point came, and I was able to understand who I was.

EMOTIONAL CPR

Another tragedy, oh, the savagery
Heart ripped out
It feels like a catastrophe.
How can I be alive but feel like I am dying inside?

Performing CPR on my life
When shit ain't going right
Universe, what is happening to me right now?

My body is tired from fighting.
The war of words trying to protect my peace
From being disturbed
But I am almost tapped out.

The mind isn't meant to be under constant distress
Internally feeling a mess
Without a solution to the heartbreak of a relationship
Death, turmoil, and depression

Anxiety to keep negative thoughts at bay.

My thoughts are obsessed with the stress of keeping $$$
in my pocket while hands are in my face asking, no,
demanding--
But the lack of understanding that this is just a job.
More compressions to my chest. I need rest, but I can't
quit; I don't want to fail—
Because if I do, I am no better than the people I work to
outdo.

But I'm only one—me
One heart, one mind
Give me two breaths before I die
I want to be alive.

But the coma I go into might feel better than the shit I am
going through
Fading fast, need to last one last breath before I see your
death...
I want to be alive...

Reflection seed:

Heartbreak is physically, mentally, and spiritually crippling. It needs just as much work as my therapists say as a cold or any type of illness/ailment. It needs room to process and heal. Along with the constant pressure I put on myself to excel at everything, I hit a wall and feel exhausted. But in the end, I didn't want to give up, I felt the chaos at the time, but I didn't want to experience it anymore.

CYCLE III: THE SUN

Smile More, Talk Less

- MY LITTLE SISTER ANGIE

ENERGIZE YOUR SPIRIT

When your spirit is weary
You have cried your pool of tears, unleashing your fears
It's time to energize your spirit
Take time to rest; you did your best

Energize your spirit so that you can live your best life
Learn to say no to the mess
Yes--- to the self-care
No-- to the negativity
Come my way, positive energy
Accept others' sympathy but don't be down too long
You are strong, and even in weakness, you still belong in this world.
Believe in yourself, create a space to have good emotional health
Energize your spirit to become the excellent human you want to be.

Reflection seed:

A moment of feeling like I would be down -- but not out and that I could get through this situation. Anxiety brought in destructive thoughts, and I faced my demons. Lots of therapy helped me breakthrough my emotional barrier of embracing who I am.

SHINE BABY

You glow in the light that no one can see
Your walk; your talk-- a spotlight
Do you have a job and your own money?
Nod your head; yes, you are blessed
Shine, baby.

An abundance of wealth
Of love, light, and purity
that only God made you be;
your spirit is free
Let the world see
Shine, baby.

Like a flower that blooms
On a rainy afternoon
You are fully grown
A mind of your own
Don't let the haters tear you down for this confidence
and happiness you have found.

Look in the mirror
You are divine
Say these words with me:
"This little light of mine, I'm going to let it shine, let it shine ... let it shine... let it shine, baby!"

Reflection seed:

A mantra and ode to a feel-good poem that is uplifting. When I wrote this, I felt like I was unstoppable. I have learned that self-motivation is the most challenging part of being human. You can cheer people on all day long with no problem, but somehow you are left in the wind.

PICK UP YOUR CROWN QUEEN (P.U.Y.C.Q)

Beautiful woman... skin smooth as butter
Mind sharp as cheddar cheese
Why don't you recognize yourself as the queen you were meant to be?
Your crown needs cleaning like jewelry, but no one can make it shine like you, baby.

Beautiful woman... hair like silk... smelling like the cocoa trees and herbs that help the forests smell serene
Look in the mirror... do you see what I see
A face that can't be erased from the hurt you feel inside
You try to hide, but I see your pain.

Beautiful woman... no one is built like you
With the power to push through all situations that make you feel small as you stand tall.
Caring for others, leaving yourself in the dust...
With no one to trust but your mind... your powerful, intelligent mind... you have come so far.

Beautiful woman... those tears are waterfalls for beauty...
Those pools of water in your eyes as you are drowning... face frowning...
Oh, girl, I see your pain... but you are brave and
These men don't deserve you.

You deserve you... because queen, you are royalty
a mother to future kings and queens...
a sister to another sister to queens...
a daughter that has to learn to spread her wings and fly...
Pick up your crown, queen.

Pick up your crown... head up, neck straight and strong
Shoulders back, you have done nothing wrong...
Walk with grace... a smile on that pretty face...
You deserve everything and more but be ready to receive
what the universe has in store.

Don't shy away...not today, these gifts you earned....
You may have been burned, but you need to heal...
That hurt you feel... that rejection you feel... that regret
you feel... The weakness you feel...
In your limbs down to the bottom of your feet
It seems like defeat...but guess what, queen
You still got your crown, queen.

Never put it down...
Another queen helps you carry it till you're ready to take
it and be proud.
No matter how life may seem...
Don't forget to
Pick up your crown, queen.

Reflection seed:

I started addressing myself as a QUEEN, and the more I embraced the royalty inside myself and how I felt I needed to be treated and how I wanted others to treat me, the more empowerment I felt in writing these words... the life around me was crashing and crumbling, but it wasn't over... I wasn't done... no, my story was far from over. This is an ode to that feeling.

HEALING PAINS

Expression in one's emotions

Like waves in the ocean, tears flow

Like a sprinkler to a plant, you can grow

I'm tired-- of those efforts for the benefit.

And still, I cry, asking why?

Why do I care and share with those who don't?

Because ...well, it's how I'm built

Frustration of progress

The path to success brings pains,

Healing pains running deep in my soul and sometimes revealed in my tone, walk, and talk.

I wish I could turn it off.

Sadness tears. It hurts me...

More than it hurts you.

Man, does that put me in my feelings;

I hate crying.

It makes me feel weak and too sad to speak, but healing hurts me.

Anger, no stranger to my internal fight, avoids an external fight with the haters, doubters, and fakers trying to stop my paper.

Damn!

Why are you worried about me? Don't you got your worry, leave me be!

Healing pains that leave no energy remain; it's draining. I'm exhausted from life's pain; I am a forgive.

I wish I reconsidered things—damn, it hurts!

It was necessary, scary, a tale of fairies, no ...no way ... not today.

I fight to stay upright, head above ground, not bowing down.

Sometimes I just want to lash out...

Nah, that ain't working out...

Now, what...oh, I know... time for healing.

Reflection seed:

The healing journey is continuous, and I learned that the expression of emotions was something I suppressed. Therapy allowed me and taught me not to compartmentalize my feelings as I had been for years. This meant saying what hurts me aloud, even to myself: asking myself what I need (Shannon would appreciate this) ... I am still a work in progress, but I have learned so much on this journey.

CYCLE IV: THE ROOTS

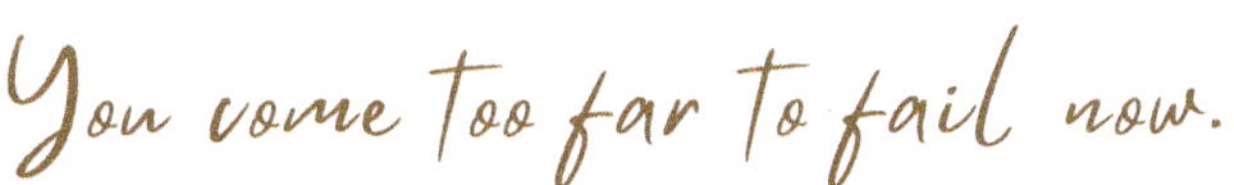

- SHARK

STRONGER

Built to last through the storm
Bond not broken, down but not out
Look in the mirror. Are you alive?
Despite the scars you feel inside, you are stronger!

Hard to get out of bed
Thoughts running in your head
Negativity saying you can't-- you won't
But lies are all I see
Weakness just ain't what you want to be!

Dark and pain-filled days
Things are not going my way, but I remain
Clouds storm only for a while
During it, you can still smile. You are stronger!

Passed over, left out but success never in doubt
Don't count me out because I am stronger!
Failure is not an option.
Choices to keep going in my heart, knowing it is tough...
but I am tougher.

Rough around the edges but still soft on the inside

Stronger, the spiritual, physical, mental battle in and
outside,

My will, the heart keeps me alive I still survive, thrive, and
drive to my destination, with no hesitation or reservation,
but I do me-- you do you-

Because I am stronger!

Reflection seed:

This poem was written when I realized that I had gone through it firm despite what I had been through. In your most challenging moments, it shows what you are made of. I was determined to be down but not stay there. I lived, and I learned.

FINDING YOUR PURPOSE

Life is hard, no really, life is hard

Obstacles at every turn

From financial to mental to physical situations leaving us feeling burned....out

Like storms turn to sunshine, snow turns to water after being melted away by the rays of a sunny day.

Your purpose is bound, waiting to be found in its time
What do you hope, dream-- aspire to be?

Not a prisoner of dire circumstances; to be given a chance to live in your purpose

Day after day, you continue to drown with an anchor weighing you down...

Time to break free

Time to get up

Time to have peace

Time to have joy.

When will it be a good time?

Anytime with life choices by design, you can decide you want happiness.

Happiness over misery

Smiles over frowns

Joy over pain

Sunshine over rain

Good times will come, but it starts with you

If you are given a chance to find your purpose...
will you?

Reflection seed:

Not many people can answer the questions "What is your purpose?" and "What is your reason for living?" because we only live to survive, including me. I needed to figure out who I was and what kept me waking up every morning. Trust me when I tell you—stick in there. It will come, for you too.

NO LOVE WITHOUT SELF LOVE

How can there be no love without self-love?

When you love others more than yourself

Self-love should be considered wealth

Something money can't buy

Yet we give it away free without anyone having to try.

Your energy should be conserved and

Preserved because protecting your peace is

Something you deserve, but it's treated like it's not a priority

King...Queen, you are royalty.

Reasons we get lonely...stay in friendships.

Marry jobs because we don't love ourselves enough to stand up for what we earned just continue to get burned

Without a care in the world... too afraid to live

More likely to die by thoughts of suicide and

No strength to survive because there is no self-love...

Self-love doesn't discriminate...it appreciates every part of you

Fat or skinny, pretty, beautiful or bright, intelligent, creative or innovative, rich or poor, tall or short...

There is no part of you that self-love doesn't enjoy, but you don't give in.

You don't accept it, yet you take mistreatment from people, knowing they are there for some seasons of your life,

Not to help you grow but to know your business...

This is a reminder that self-love can't wait another day for you to decide if it's something you need to survive when you know dang well it is what you need to prepare for your journey...

Whatever you're stuck in... it's not forever, but it only works if you hold yourself together...

I can't do it...
Your mom, husband, family, family, friends, coworkers can love you more than you love you...

It shouldn't even be a competition, but you allow others to bully you into submission,

Sacrificing and paying the price when self-love is how you live your life.

I'd love to take the burden off you, but it's a battle meant for you to go through if you don't figure it out...

Then it's gonna be a long road for you to walk out, but I believe in you...

When no one else wants to...

Self-love is the cure for the hurt, the broken heart bleeding from scars...

Allowing you to protect yourself is your best defense... I hope this all makes sense.

Self-love is quiet time; peace of mind; it is just what it says:

Loving oneself.

It wasn't always clear to me, but now that I know, I want to tell you that you have this, too, based on what I have been through

Battle scars are seen to the eye, and those you don't see...

That I'm still healing, and you can too...

Because there is no love without self-love.

Reflection seed:

A turning point in my life and one of my most powerful pieces-- when I realized that I hadn't been taking care of myself while pouring into everyone else. Emotions came out, and that is when I decided I wanted to do more poetry and use it as part of my therapy. Self-love isn't always taught or learned-- I am still a work in progress and continuously working to make myself better mentally, spiritually, and emotionally.

REFLECTIVE POWER

The mirror is showing me myself
Depths of what I never felt
This is my reflection, and no perfection
Of a sight seen-- yet unseen.

Looking in, not looking back
Because the mirror has reflective power
Showing different faces in different spaces
Yet the same face but different levels of emotions
To be happy, sad mad is all reflective power
How people may see you and how you see you is perspective.

A broken mirror reflects multiple faces yet still all in one soul
This means being broken doesn't change the space or who you are In your face
It's a tool of reflection...just like a dirty mirror can be cleaned and clear
I need all of you to understand that it's nothing to fear in this.

It's the power to confront yourself without hesitation; it doesn't go away because you look out...

The mirror still shows you what it sees
A power that shouldn't be taken lightly can show you sides that you may not have seen.

A broken mirror still reflects
A dirty mirror still reflects
Cleaning the mirror clears for you to see
The person you are to what the eye can see.

There is power in reflection, so be wise to treat yourself,

Respect yourself and check yourself on what the reflective power ultimately means.

Reflection seed:

I would post notes with quotes of positive affirmations on my mirror because looking at myself in the mirror wasn't associated with positive thinking. I was obsessed with physical appearance versus my emotional health. Learning to love myself started with looking at different sayings from various people in my life that I love, respect, admire, and some that I don't know but just appreciate their words. The mirror has power; how you view yourself can project onto others. I learned how to change my reflective management by paying more attention to how I viewed myself.

CYCLE V:
THE SUNFLOWER

*Love the good days, accept the bad days..
Finf ways to overcome in a healthy,
loving way that works for you*

- SHANNON

GROW LIKE A SUNFLOWER

A sunflower takes 80 to 120 days to fully mature
To reach 12 feet of growth in just three months
Yet we give ourselves less time to heal or grieve,
Fail or celebrate what we achieve.

A sunflower shows us that in different stages
In our life, we can grow tall
Starting with planting the seed in our life just
Like doubts and fear, it stays in our mind till
Something else appears like strength and courage
Confidence and high self-esteem.

The second stage is germination, as the flower
Grows into seedlings...its life is awakened
Maybe right now, it doesn't feel like you are
Awakened, but you start with the seedling of belief
Taking that one step out of bed when you
Don't feel like you can in your head, but you can!

The third stage is leaf development.
Where you notice two leaves appear from what
It started as a seed... not everything you are
Doing beneath the soil needs to be revealed
Because it's for you to experience until you
Feel ready to show your growth.

The fourth stage is a growing bud ...not quite a
Flower yet, but it's coming soon, love
Just hold on and be patient...
That work you have been putting in
It is not too far away, that financial struggle
You have been in won't be a struggle soon.

The fifth stage is flowering with the petals.
Opening stretching far enough to receive the sunlight
Your time to shine you waited long enough
And it's your time!

The sixth stage is pollination, as the bees come.
And want to receive what your growth has been
anticipated ...meaning others can learn
From your experience
Pollinating others in similar situations, spreading growth.

The seventh stage is seed development...you know.
Those sunflower seeds in the bags from the grocery store
with
Different flavors and learning to savor the hard work of
that growth

The eighth stage is when you can be great at harvesting
You can feed others the seeds or spread the seeds
Throughout the winter, where they can bloom when it's
their season.

This isn't about a sunflower; it's about how a seed can
grow into something truly remarkable.
Plant your seed
Nurture your soul
Embrace your stems
Bloom from your bud
And pollinate those around you so they can be great
Because tomorrow isn't promised, but neither is today.

Reflection seed:

I remember deciding I liked sunflowers when I went to a sunflower field and was constantly surrounded by these tall, beautiful plants. I cut a few and took them home, but they didn't live long; I didn't invest in caring for them. Then, I decided to get some seeds from the store and plant my own, and that's when I became invested. Over time my affection grew, and since then, I have fallen in love with this flower and its strength and height. It has been an inspiration for my personal development and growth ever since.

HAIR I TAGE

An afro... growing to the heavens.

Spreading its roots like a tree

Hair-- the best visual form of versatility

Do you wear your hair like a crown on your head, like a queen or king with the power to be art to the eyes of anyone who sees...?

Your hair is laid.

Be proud; you are royalty with the ability to diversify your braids, weaves, waves, and two-strand twists in so many different ways, or

Maybe you are more relaxed...

As madame C. J. Walker paved the way to be a self-made millionaire off of Hair I Tage.

Oh, there are more who laid the path...like Lydia Newman, creator of the hairbrush...

For those curls, knots, hard-to-reach spots...a pioneer...

Christina Jenkins, the key to sewing in the weave to have locks like Lauryn Hill short or long...

A protective style or Carol Randal, concerned about the burns by the relaxer, created the ear clips to protect our pretty faces

and even to flat-iron the shorter strands...

It separates sections having hair pressed to perfection...
what an invention!

Who is to define whether it matters if the hair is mine...?

I own it... using my styles to flaunt it...

Look, but don't touch... it's called respecting the art...
The form...the human being...

Can you appreciate seeing it through your eyes...
God's creation?

The term nappy is not a compliment. It's a name that
seems to frame a lack of being able to tame your
crown... what about kinky...?

What about a hair type? Does it matter... do you love it?
Is it yours?

Then walk... strut... command presence into that room...
As your hair continues to bloom like that flower

Diversify your spectrum...look through a color wheel of
lenses to see that your black and brown friends struggle
to fit in...

Welcome them with love... if you treat their hair like a
science project at the fair...

it's demeaning... just read and learn what it means only to
be heard

But not seen...

That hair is a part of being human

So, I say that we must educate and appreciate the pioneers that gave us gifts to the growth of hair...

The many styles we wear... as we love it no matter the texture color...

Take a moment...

Learn and thank the ancestors of what we like to call Hair I Tage.

Reflection seed:

I have been natural with my hair (no relaxers or chemicals) since 2012, and my hair has become a part of my identity. Sometimes it's hard for others to see, and I needed to pay homage to the inventors who created the tools to do my hair. This is my way of gratitude.

LIFE IS PRECIOUS

You don't know if you will wake up tomorrow.

If today is your last day to say .... "I love you," "I forgive you," "I'm sorry."

To those close to you because life is a gift to be treasured beyond measure with every last breath in your lungs till your day is done

Life is precious.

Don't leave words unsaid before you get news that the person is gone, and what you put off for years can never be revealed.

The anger and hatred you hold are waiting to be released so you can have peace.

It's time to let it go like Keyshia Cole; regret, fear, and sadness need to be unleashed to avoid the madness.
Life is precious.

Say that apology, forgive... express the sadness and emotion, and don't wait before it's too late...

That last word you say seals fate before you change this...
Rebuild that relationship, heal that friendship

You and the other person can do this...

Be the bigger person because life could be taken in a second.

Life is precious.

Reflection seed:

During COVID, many deaths occurred, including famous and non-famous... close friends and distant friends--affecting everyone. It started to feel normal and made me realize that life is too short, as they say, but even more, Life is precious. I was taught in therapy about gratitude and being grateful on top of making sure to thank myself for things, the simple things, appreciating the simple things, and most importantly, bringing perspective to those around me.

ABOUT THE AUTHOR

Andrea is a first-time author but has been creative writing for a few years. Her love of poetry has drawn her to do spoken word all around Texas, including Poetry on the Patio and Beatstreet. With her adulthood journey of 19 years, she has experienced plenty and has dealt with anxiety and P.T.S.D, but that hasn't stopped her from producing poems as a form of therapy. The Seeds of a Sunflower: Poems of Growth captures the journey and experiences that she has gone through in her first book.

ACKNOWLEDGMENTS

This book wouldn't have come to fruition if it wasn't for The Coalition, family, friends, "Mitch," my therapist, mentors, and coaches-- among others in my life. May I continue to be inspired by all of you and your lives, synchronizing with mine to be a better person?

Additionally, my team made this book what it is as you read this. After many discussions with my editor and the voice of reason, Umar, who helped anchor my journey in more ways than one. I appreciate you as I like to call you "book bestie." Jennifer, for the mentoring on how this process works and helping me believe I can self-publish. Kiki, for the blurb, wow, what a fantastic writer! Belmma from Plan B Dsgn for the cover design, and chapter design, you are a gem, and I can't wait to work with you again!

To the reader of this book, I hope that you understand my journey and that it resonates with your spirit.

ABOUT THIS BOOK

Every sunflower seed can grow into a new flower.

Like love overcoming trauma, self-worth emerging from self-doubt, or a new purpose stumbled upon after an identity crisis; each sunflower seed will bloom and grow.

It will eventually be reborn with enough care and nurturing if you bury it deep enough.

Seeds of a Sunflower is a thought-provoking, raw collection of autobiographical poems that will break your heart and piece it back together, petal by petal, leaf by leaf, existing parasites and thorns included.

By exposing this vulnerable, private side of her, Andrea Conn tackles the shame and stigma society associates with trauma, loss, paralyzing fear, and imperfection. Her struggles with PTSD, infertility, and personal identity—a daily relatable battle that countless people face—illuminate the slow, painful path to inner strength and self-love.

The sunflower will stand tall again. The phoenix will rise from its ashes. The wounds will fade into scars.

You won't forget how long it took you to heal, how much recovery resembled heartbreak, and how it hurt to grow again.

Because you are worth more than you can imagine!

www.ingramcontent.com/pod-product-compliance
Ingram Content Group UK Ltd.
Pitfield, Milton Keynes, MK11 3LW, UK
UKHW021839270726
14058UKWH00002B/238

9 798218 110512